ALL YOU NEED TO KNOW....

HOW TO WRITE WELL

BY TIM DE LISLE

Leabharlanna Poibli Chathair Baile Atha Cliath
Dublin City Public Libraries

CONTENTS

Don't be afraid to dip in ...

10 9 8 7 6 5 4 3 2 1

ISBN 978-1-911187-90-5
First published as *All you need to know: How to Write Well*
by Connell Publishing in 2018

Picture credits:
Cover illustration © NatBasil / Shutterstock
pp. 3, 14, 26, 36, 53, 57, 59, 63, 72, 74, 78 © Nick Newman

Copyright © 2018 by Tim De Lisle
Design: Ben Brannan
Associate Publisher: Paul Woodward
Edited by Jolyon Connell
Assistant Editor and typeset by Alfred Fletcher

Printed in Great Britain

INTRODUCTION

Writing matters. We all do it, and we all admire it when it's done well. It doesn't just express us: it represents us. It is there, on someone else's screen, when we are not there. Writing is the second most important thing we learn at school, after how to get along with others – and it helps with that too.

When we are seven, writing is fun, absorbing, creative, like painting or dressing up. Somewhere along the steep ascent of the next ten years, that feeling can be lost, stifled by school or smothered by self-consciousness. This slim volume aims to bring the fun back, by showing you simple ways to write better. It's not the last word on the subject; it's a quick guide, packed with tips picked up in my life as a writer and editor.

One reason why our love of writing wilts is that it doesn't get much watering. Teachers often have their eye on something else, and perhaps (whisper it) they were never taught to write well themselves. Writing is like dancing, in that you can tell instantly if someone is good at it. But it's also like driving, in that it can be taught. If you find it hard, you're in good company: even some famous writers rely rather too heavily on their editors.

Writing is not about being a genius; few people are. It's wonderful when you see it elevated to an art, but most of the time it's just a craft. The question isn't whether you are a born writer. It's whether there is a better writer inside you, waiting to get out.

Any writing, anywhere, can be good, bad, or somewhere in between. There are tweets that are beautifully composed and trilogies that are terrible. A line jotted inside a birthday card can be just right – warm, funny or loving. A three-word slogan can be inspired, as the Conservative Party famously showed in 1979 with "Labour isn't working", or it can be drivel, as the Trainline booking service helpfully confirmed in 2016 with "i am train".

Writing will help you cope with exams, but that's not really the point. It helps you cope with life. A well-written email can land you a job; a well-written text can seal a friendship or start a romance. All you need is an open mind, a supply of energy, and the desire to improve.

Books of advice on anything are apt to be irritating, and rare is the piece of writing about good writing that doesn't end up offering examples of bad writing itself. You probably know Murphy's Law, the pessimist's charter which states that whatever can go wrong, will go wrong. Writers of books like this mutter darkly about Murphy's lesser-known twin, Muphry's law, which states that anyone who criticises someone else's writing or editing will commit some howler of their own. Your job is to see if you can spot it; mine is to apologise in advance.

You can read the book from start to finish in a couple of hours, or you can just dip in. I hope you find it useful, and entertaining.

Chapter 1

BE CLEAR

One summer, nearly a lifetime ago, a leaflet came through the door of every household in Britain. It brought news of something quietly revolutionary.

> **Your new National Health Service begins on 5th July. What is it? How do you get it?**
>
> It will provide you with all medical, dental and nursing care. Everyone – rich or poor, man, woman or child – can use it or any part of it. There are no charges, except for a few special items. There are no insurance qualifications. But it is not a "charity". You are all paying for it, mainly as tax payers, and it will relieve your money worries in time of illness.

If medals were handed out for services to clarity, the anonymous authors of these words would have got one. They kept it magnificently simple.

First, they announced the launch of an institution, in the plainest language, stating its name and giving its start date, and choosing "begin" rather than its pompous brother "commence", which often proves irresistible to officials. Then they asked two questions: "What is it? How do you get it?" All the best questions are short, because then they are big and open, leaving room for many different answers. And this even applies, as here, with a question you ask yourself.

So far we've had three sentences but only 16 words, none of them long. This is plain speaking, which inspires trust: it tells us that the authors have nothing to hide.

The sentences that follow, giving the answers, are almost as short as the questions. Every clause is a main clause, entire and of itself. The first sentence sums up what the NHS offers: "It will provide you with all medical, dental and nursing care." The second spells out who it's for: "Everyone – rich or poor, man, woman or child – can use it or any part of it." The third sentence says that nearly all of this new service will be free; the fourth assures you that you don't need insurance. The fifth sentence ("But it is not a 'charity'") and the first half of the sixth ("You are all paying for it") show how the service is funded, and the paragraph finishes with the emotional impact that is the point of the whole exercise – peace of mind. "It will relieve your money worries in time of illness." The worries are not specified, but the person picking the leaflet up off the doormat can fill in the blank: they will be free from a vicious double whammy – having cancer, say, and finding that they can't afford the treatment they need. (In America, where there is still no NHS, it's reported that medical bills bankrupt 643,000 people every year.)

All this is done calmly, crisply, with no fuss or grandstanding. Which is not to say that it's flawless. A picky editor might have trimmed a couple of words: "can use it or any part of it" might have flowed better, and meant the same, as "can use any part of it". "Qualifications" is jarring, a word of five syllables in a paragraph where everything else has three at most: that sentence would have been plainer and simpler as "You don't need insurance". And there's another bum note in the quote marks around "charity". The point being made here is straightforwardly true – the NHS is not a charity – so there's no need to complicate things with quotes. The full stop after "charity" could have been a colon, to show the link with the next clause, and the comma after "tax payers" could have been a full stop. The "you" at the start of the next sentence could have been a "we" (rule of thumb: don't address your audience in the plural, as you're trying to connect with each one), and "mainly as tax payers" could have been a touch simpler – "through our taxes". But this is still a paragraph of immense power. It contains only 88 words, yet it conveys all the main points about a new institution. It is direct, helpful and down-to-earth.

I have a friend who, unlike me, was alive to witness the birth of the NHS – he was 19 then, and he's 89 as these words are being written. His name is Irving Wardle and he's a theatre critic, best known for spotting Harold Pinter. When they were both young men, Pinter started writing plays and Irving put his finger on what they were like, calling them "comedies of menace", a phrase that has now been circulating for nearly half a century. So when he says something about the language, it carries weight. Irving came to the launch of the first edition of this book, in 2017, and sent me an email afterwards. "I spotted your National Health quote as a model of English prose," he wrote. "So true. It deserves a place alongside the Gettysburg Address."

Clarity is, among other things, a courtesy. It means using words the reader will understand, which means using words you understand yourself. Being clear is far more important than being clever. If you can be both at once, all the better; but it's not worth going out of your way to sound clever, because it hardly ever works. An outstanding TV critic, Nancy Banks-Smith, once said, "We cannot put pen to paper without revealing something of ourselves." When we get caught trying to look clever, we just end up looking foolish. Next time you're tempted to use a word you don't understand, ask yourself this: do you want to look like a 12-year-old with a cigarette?

If the temptation persists, all you have to do is look the word up. Real writers have a dictionary to hand, and they're not fussed whether it's on paper or online, as long as it's authoritative. You can't go wrong with the Concise Oxford Dictionary, the Collins English Dictionary, or Dictionary.com, which began in 1995 (before Google) and relies on the Random House Unabridged Dictionary. If a word is too new or too slangy for those august pages, it may well have landed at urbandictionary.com, which is just as enlightening and more likely to make you laugh.

One reason the NHS leaflet worked was that it had a strong sense of its reader. It wasn't aimed at the educated; it could be understood by anyone who was able to read, and by many people who weren't, because the short sentences made it easy to read aloud to the illiterate, or to children – a bigger consideration then than it is now, but still worth bearing in mind. The authors didn't let their phrasing get in the way of their meaning. Consciously or not, they complied with a famous maxim coined two years earlier, in 1946, by George Orwell: "Good prose is like a windowpane."

Orwell believed, with a passion, that the powerful need to be straight with us. He would have groaned had he lived to see the day when Theresa May made her first comment on the news that she was going to be Britain's prime minister. "I'm humbled," she said, when she meant the exact opposite – I'm honoured, I'm proud. And this was someone who had advertised herself as straight-talking. Many people won't have been bothered by it, but some will have heard it as an alarm bell, a sign that they needed to keep an ear on her.

Clarity breeds credibility. May's catchphrase, if any, is "I have been very clear that..." She was still trotting it out two years later, when she still hadn't been clear about the most important choice facing her: what form she wanted Brexit to take – soft or hard, expensive or ruinous, the Norway solution or the Canada one. (And, as some wag said, there's only one thing between Norway and Canada: the wreck of the Titanic.)

It may well be that "humbled" is in the process of changing its meaning. Boris Johnson, who is far more of a wordsmith than May, used it the same way, the very next day. Language is a democracy and, as both of them had just seen, democracies can make funny decisions.

Even if you're not powerful, it's vital to say what you mean (unless you're cracking a joke, which may involve saying the exact opposite). Just as sports people speak of treating their sport with respect, so anyone who writes anything needs to show some respect to the language. Words have a certain logic built into them. They mean what they are agreed to mean, which isn't always what we want them to mean. Our job is to find the words that say what we mean. Ambiguity can be highly effective – especially in a song, a poem or a story – but it's a weapon to add to your arsenal after making a habit of being clear. First learn the rules, then think about breaking them. Even Andy Warhol, who became famous by making screenprints of photographs of celebrities, had learned to draw.

YOUR TURN

Being as clear and direct as you can...

a) Invent a game and explain the rules or

b) Invent a job and apply for it

WHAT FOOTBALL PUNDITS SAY, AND WHAT THEY MEAN

Owen Hargreaves, commentating on Real Madrid v Man City, 4 May 2016:
What he said: *"If that's not a foul, I'll never know."*
What he meant: *"If that's not a foul, I don't know what is."*

Glenn Hoddle, commentating on England v Turkey, 22 May:
What he said: *"It's a great time to hit the manager in the eye."*
What he meant: *"It's a great time to catch the manager's eye."*

Robbie Savage, reflecting on England v Wales, 16 June:
What he said: *"Wales will fight to live another day."*
What he meant: *"Wales will live to fight another day."*

Steve McManaman, commentating on Leicester v Man Utd, 7 August:
What he said: *"Leicester not changing anything they didn't do last season."*
What he meant: *"Leicester not doing anything they didn't do last season."*

WRITERS ON WRITING

'A word after a word after a word is power.'
Margaret Atwood

'My task, by the power of the written word, is to make you hear, to make you feel – it is, before all, to make you see.'
Joseph Conrad

'True ease in writing comes from art, not chance, As those move easiest who have learn'd to dance.'
Alexander Pope

'Writing is the art of applying the ass to the seat.'
Dorothy Parker

'Substitute "damn" every time you're inclined to write "very"; your editor will delete it and the writing will be just as it should be.'
Mark Twain

'This letter is longer than usual, because I've not had time to make it shorter.'
Blaise Pascal

'If you don't have time to read, you don't have the time — or the tools — to write. Simple as that.'
Stephen King

I WISH THEY'D GET TO THE POINT!
WAFFLE RECIPE

Chapter 2

BE CONCISE

Brevity, Polonius says in *Hamlet*, is the soul of wit. It's an all-time great line, nonchalantly practising what it preaches, while also poking fun at Polonius himself for being long-winded. You could even go a step further and argue that brevity is the soul of writing. The words you write are going to bite into your reader's time, so it's good manners not to be greedy – and sound tactics too, because waffle, while delicious for breakfast, is tiresome on the page. And readers, especially teachers and examiners, can spot it a mile off.

Every so often, someone somewhere launches a short-story competition in which the story has to be told in six words. The most famous example is attributed to Ernest Hemingway: "For sale, baby shoes, never worn". Whoever it's by, it could hardly be better. It has the element of surprise, and uses it – as Flaubert said about the aspirations of writers in general – to move the stars to pity.

Twitter, in its early years, was sometimes dismissed as being dumbed-down because of its 140-character limit. Yet the baby-shoes story would have fitted into a tweet, no trouble. Here's an actual tweet, posted on 10 June 2016, which also tells a story, albeit one that was, at the time, set in the future.

> **Robert Harris** @ Robert___Harris
>
> Scenario: Leave win. PM resigns. Boris leader. No majority for Brexit in Commons. Autumn election to seek mandate. Tories split. Then what?

Harris is a political novelist who used to be a political correspondent, and you can see him drawing on both those careers here, as he packs six predictions into his 140 characters. Harris, writing before the referendum had even taken place, got an awful lot right. He could have made his point at a leisurely pace in a think-piece for one of the papers, but by putting it straight on Twitter, he gave it extra punch and urgency, and saved himself a fair amount of time.

Twitter, while not always good for social harmony, does us a favour by forcing us to do something we should be doing anyway as we write: to distil our thoughts. Sometimes this is just a matter of finding the right word, and not using four or five of them where one will do. If you're tempted to write "despite the fact that", bear in mind that we already have a word for that: "although". "Increase the size of": try "increase" on its own, or one of its sisters – "enlarge" or "expand". "At this moment in time": how about "now"? On a British Airways transatlantic flight in 2018, the bread roll came with something called Fresh Buttery Taste Spread. In your kitchen, let there be butter.

In language, as in deciding what to wear, there are some frills that are not worth having. "Amongst" adds nothing to "among" apart from a whiff of pretension, and it's the same with "whilst" and "while". The extra letters sit there like a pair of spats, making you look, by modern standards, mildly ridiculous.

That said, it's possible to take compression too far. Writing can become too staccato if it's just one short sentence after another. Advice, especially, can be too bald: "do not be hectoring or arrogant," the Economist Style Guide once said, making a perfectly valid point in a way which, as one reviewer pointed out, is quite hectoring and arrogant itself. And now that long-distance communication has gone back to the written word, there are few characters in life more maddening than the friend whose texts or DMs are relentlessly terse. As a rule of thumb, it helps to start and finish any personal communication with a thought that is all about the other person, however mundane ("hope you're very well", "thinking of you", "best of luck tomorrow"). If you get into a rapid exchange of news, views or something more flirtatious, this rule is suspended in the middle. It's like playing tennis: you need to make sure your opponent is ready for a serve, but you don't need to worry once the

WE NEED TO TALK ABOUT... PERFECTIONISM

The point of re-reading and re-writing isn't to achieve perfection. There's no such thing. For a couple of years, on The Independent on Sunday, I had the pleasure of editing Anthony Lane, who went on to join the New Yorker and become probably the most admired film critic writing today.

When he collected his film reviews in a book, in 2002, he called it *Nobody's Perfect*. He was quoting the famous final line of *Some Like It Hot*, uttered by the idiotic millionaire Osgood Fielding III, on being told by his new girlfriend that she is, in fact, a man. Inside the jokey reference there's a grain of seriousness. No writer is perfect, not even the all-time greats. Shakespeare can be try-hard, Austen can be long-winded, Dickens can be silly, and Orwell can be plain wrong. The expression "word-perfect" is close to being an oxymoron.

Perfectionism is a neurosis – an understandable one, but one that is apt to drive people mad. By all means use it as a spur to make your writing better, up to a point. You'll know when you reach that point, because your changes will be mere tinkering and the thing you've written will be going round in circles. Take the hint, leave the screen – walk the dog, wash the dishes, phone a friend.

rally is under way.

There are two kinds of padding that are particularly worth watching out for. One is saying the same thing twice; in an effort not to do it myself, I'll be expanding on that in Chapter 6. The other is self-consciousness, the curse of our heavily mediated age. Self-awareness is a strength, self-consciousness a pain, and it's all too easy to tip over from one to the other. A simple way to avoid it is this: don't mention yourself unless you have to. If tempted to comment on yourself, resist the temptation and leave it to others, who often judge us more gently anyway. Doing yourself down, while more endearing than bigging yourself up – and certainly more English – involves grabbing the same amount of limelight.

Leaving yourself out of it, if you can, is worth doing even in small ways. If you've written "I think", or "I would say that", or "I have come to the conclusion that", try the same sentence without it. At a stroke, it will be not just more concise, but more confident.

Just beyond self-consciousness, two more rocks lie in wait: self-obsession and self-delusion. "I think I'm actually humble," Donald Trump told an interviewer on American television in July 2016. "I think I'm much more humble than you would understand." If he was really humble, (a) he wouldn't say so, and (b) he wouldn't pre-

THE DOS AND DON'TS OF DON'T AND WON'T

"Don't", "won't" and "can't", "he's" and "she's" and "they're" are all fine – they save a syllable, they get us to the point quicker, they feel natural and they've long since become part of the furniture. If someone disapproves of them, you could gently ask whether they disapprove of "goodbye" too, on the grounds that it started life as "God be with you".

Contractions shouldn't be compulsory: there are times when we can do with the extra muscle of the separate words ("Do not pass Go", "You cannot be serious"). And you may choose to mix the two modes: "It is well known that a vital ingredient of success is not knowing that what you're attempting can't be done" (Terry Pratchett, *Equal Rites*, 1987).

The only contractions to steer clear of are "would've", "could've" and "should've": they look clunky and save no syllables, because they sound just the same as the words they're trying to replace.

sume that the interviewer wouldn't understand. If he was concise, he wouldn't have bothered saying "I think" once, let alone twice. Once he became president, Trump's utterances were so bad – so full of rubbish, racism, boasting and attempted bullying – that they could be used as a model of how not to express yourself.

On the whole, it's better just to say things than to say things about the things you are saying. Even a phrase like "Put simply" can be irritating: putting things simply is great, as we've seen, but commenting on it may have the reader groaning and muttering "get on with it". Phrases like "It would be no exaggeration to say that…" contain more than their share of hot air. As Oscar Wilde almost said, it's the importance of being not too earnest.

YOUR TURN

Emulating Ernest Hemingway (above), write your own very short story – in six words if you can, but feel free to stretch to 12. If you're on Twitter, or know someone who is, send it to me @TimdeLisle.

WHY WRITE?

At times, as you plod through another essay or email, you may wonder what writing is for. It's a question that might elicit a hundred different answers. Mine goes like this.

We write to connect with other people – to make them laugh, or cry, or think.

We also write to work out what we think ourselves: there's nothing like it for concentrating the mind. Don DeLillo writes big fat novels and looks as if he's got it all worked out, but he once said: "I don't know what I think about certain subjects, even today, until I sit down and try to write about them." That's a nice "try".

We write to tell a story, to capture a truth, to persuade, or to entertain. It could be an email or an essay, a letter, a job application, or the dreaded personal statement for university. Writing isn't just writing, it's doing. It can show gratitude, cement a relationship, boost our chances of getting on in life.

We write to express ourselves. A couple of years ago I reported on the charity First Story, which sets up after-school writing groups led by authors (general idea: have a biscuit, write a poem). The students' self-esteem rose as they displayed a talent they hadn't known they possessed. And it's not just self-esteem. Our writing represents us when we're not there; it can give a good impression of us or a bad one. Not all these lights are switched on all the time, but they never go out all at once.

NOT A HIP WAS WRIGGLED...

The book that did most to inspire this one is *Put it in Writing* (1984) by John Whale, a guide so crisp and wise that every intern I ever hired ended up reading it. Early on, Whale champions this passage from *Pax Brittanica* (1968) by James Morris (now Jan Morris), showing what Sundays were like in a border town in Canada in the 1890s.

> The bars, theatres and dance halls closed at a minute before midnight every Saturday night, and not a whisky was sold again, not a hip was wriggled, not a bet was placed, until two in the morning on Monday. The Sunday sounds of Dawson City were psalms and snores. No kind of work was allowed. Men were arrested for fishing on a Sunday, or for sawing wood. The only hope of living it up, between Saturday night and Monday morning, was to take a boat downriver and slip across the line into the States – out of reach of the Pax Britannica and its stern schoolmarm values.

A less sparky writer might have said something like this. "Sundays in Dawson City were sacrosanct, reserved for going to church or going to sleep. The residents were not allowed to dance, gamble, buy alcohol, go fishing or even do any work, unless they crossed the border into the United States, out of reach of the British Empire and its Victorian values."

That would have summed up the situation solidly enough and saved 60 words or so, but it would have deprived us of the whisky, the hip, the wriggle, the bet, the psalms, the snores, the fishing, the sawing and the boat, not to mention the bars, the theatres, the dance halls and the precise timings. It would have drained the colour from the passage, and much of the life: there would have been hardly anything to see or hear or smell or feel – let alone remember.

Morris's paragraph isn't difficult or demanding. The pace is quick, the words are short, the tone is informal, and yet there's some shape. All those sights and sounds are there to work up to the main point, which uses the title of the book and punches it home with one well-chosen word – "schoolmarm". It's like watching a string of passes, wondering where they're going, and then seeing the ball in the back of the net. To write well, John Whale says, "you should think in pictures, write as you speak, and keep your reader happy". This passage does all of that.

YOUR TURN

1. When sorrows come, they come not in single spies/ But in battalions. – **Shakespeare,** *Hamlet*

Think of another vivid way to show that troubles seem to turn up in clusters.

2. Don't tell me the moon is shining; show me the glint of light on broken glass. – **Anton Chekhov**

Find a vivid way to end these two sentences:

(a) Don't tell me it's raining; show me...

(b) Don't tell me you went on holiday; show me...

3. Read this passage from *Charlie and the Chocolate Factory* (1964) by **Roald Dahl**:

Charlie Bucket stared around the gigantic room in which he now found himself. The place was like a witch's kitchen! All about him black metal pots were boiling and bubbling on huge stoves, and kettles were hissing and pans were sizzling, and strange iron machines were clanking and spluttering, and there were pipes running all over the ceiling and walls, and the whole place was lled with smoke and steam and delicious rich smells.

Then think of a room, real or imagined, and try to have as much fun describing it as Dahl did there.

GOOD TO SEE THE IMPROVEMENT IN SPELLING AND PUNCTUATION
ST JUDE'S ACADEMY
DOWN WITH SCHOOL!
TEACHERS SMELL
THE HEAD' S A MUPPET!

Chapter 3

BE VIVID

At the risk of stating the bleeding obvious, writing is an activity. George Mackay Brown, an author of great character who lived on Orkney off the north coast of Scotland, used to say that a writer was like any other worker, a farmer or a carpenter or a plumber. It may not look this way to anyone wandering past as you sit there and stare at your screen, but you are making something. You need to bring plenty of energy to the task. Read a page by the columnist Caitlin Moran and see how much effort she puts into each paragraph. You won't write well if you're distracted or dopey: the writing gods expect you to be switched on. This doesn't mean resorting to cups of tea or cans of Red Bull – just making sure you're concentrating, if only for half an hour. Treat it as a series of sprints at first, and you should soon find yourself in the 800 metres.

If you're switched on, your sentences are more likely to be the third thing they most need to be, after clear and concise: vivid.

Bad writing lands dead on the page, whereas good writing is alive. And what gives it life, more often than not, is that it is visual. A picture may be worth a thousand words, but those thousand words can contain a multitude of pictures. There's no literary mantra more vital than "show and tell", and it's no accident that "show" comes first. Good writers give examples, make things concrete, engage our eyes and ears, take something mundane or middling and make it memorable. Many of us have observed at some time or other that things, especially bad things, seem to happen in clusters, but only Shakespeare, writing *Hamlet* in about 1600, put it like this: "When sorrows come, they come not single spies. But in battalions." And only Neil Gaiman, in his novel *Neverwhere* (1996), put it like this: "Richard had noticed that events were cowards: they didn't occur singly, but instead they would run in packs and leap out at him all at once". The observation may be an obvious one, but Shakespeare and Gaiman transform it by adding vividness. Like a friend visiting a family and turning up with a present for the children, they bring something eye-catching: the spies and the cowards.

Ever since team games took off and nation started playing against nation, the thought has occurred to people that sport has a certain amount in common with war. But it took George Orwell to crystallise it: "Sport is war minus the shooting." Many people have sat around a table in a group and seen it come to the wrong decision, but only one of them, long since lost in the mists of time, put it like this: "A camel is a horse designed by a committee." There's a school of thought that this was cruel to camels, just as the ex-ghostwriter who said of Donald Trump, "I put lipstick on a pig", should surely have received a lawsuit from the sty. But writing doesn't have a duty to be inarguably right. It just has a duty to encapsulate things, and the pig and the camel play their parts.

One of the best-loved novels of the 21st century, *Wolf Hall,* retells the tale of Henry VIII through the eyes of Thomas Cromwell. Hilary Mantel could have begun with Cromwell's first day working for Henry, or his first brush with Anne Boleyn; instead she starts years earlier, with Cromwell as a teenager, in Putney, being beaten up by his own father. Or rather lying in the gutter, straight afterwards. "I heard a voice saying 'Now get up'," Mantel told an audience of 700 at the Union Chapel in Islington in 2014. This was the voice of Cromwell's father, reeking of contempt, untroubled by remorse, let alone love. "And then all the decisions about the novel had been made." It can't have been that easy, but it makes a good story. And it's striking that Mantel opens with the incident that gives her Cromwell his motivation.

Something else she said that night sticks in the memory. "People suppose that imagination is an airy quality, and that employing it is a genteel act that might be done on a chaise longue. But to imagine properly, you have to imagine strenuously. It involves your whole body, from feet to head." So creative writing is closer to acting than we might think. At that talk, Mantel was sharing the stage with an actress, Harriet Walter. And, even in saying this, she was putting her arguments into pictures – the whole body, the head and the feet, and, best of all the chaise longue, with its air of useless affluence.

Sometimes you need to do the telling before the showing, to set up a good line. In Alan Bennett's *The History Boys*, a wonderful play but one that is almost as male as its name suggests, the nearest thing to a female lead is Mrs Lintott, the teacher who is the voice of reason, practicality, scepticism and feminism. "History," she proclaims, "is a commentary on the various and continuing incapabilities of men." Which, by Bennett's high standards, is rather a dry sentence, all abstract nouns and no pictures. But we soon discover that it's only the set-up. "What is history?" Mrs Lintott goes on. "History is women following behind with the bucket." At the time, in 2006, this got a big laugh; ten years later, when Theresa May moved into Downing Street to clear up the mess left by David Cameron, Boris Johnson, Michael Gove and Nigel Farage, it was looking prophetic too.

Here are a few more ways to be vivid.

Be conversational

It will make your writing intelligible, digestible, enjoyable. You'll have to be selective at the same time – pure conversation, with its ums and ers and likes and innits, doesn't work on the page, except (obviously) as dialogue. But it's easy to lurch too far the other way. Fine writing has less to do with formality than people assume. Homer, the first great writer in the Western world, was an epic poet, yet he was described by Matthew Arnold, a Victorian professor of poetry, as "eminently rapid… eminently plain and direct". *Hamilton*, the latest musical to be acclaimed as a classic, is deliciously conversational. Lin-Manuel Miranda has written a history play about a real person from the 18th century that is unmistakably contemporary. "We hold these truths to be self-evident that all men are created equal," sings Hamilton's sister-in-law, Angelica, in a song called The Schuyler Sisters. Miranda deserves a medal just for fitting that line to music, but he has more. "When I meet Thomas Jefferson," Angelica goes on, "I'm-a compel him to include women in the sequel." Coming straight after Jefferson, that "I'm-a" captures the collisions – between past and present, white and black, rigidity and diversity – that the play is all about.

Switching from talking to writing is like getting ready for a night out. You're not putting on fancy dress, or trying to look like someone else; you're going as yourself, but making more effort, being a bit smarter, getting closer to your best.

Give your vocab an upgrade

We all have our favourite words, and the reader will soon tire of them. Whole societies have their favourites too. In the English language in the 21st century, "literally" and "genuinely" have joined the club of words that act as social glue. But they won't do much for your writing. "Literally", in a piece of writing, leans back towards its original meaning – "not figuratively" – so it will work with that hat on, but not as an all-purpose form of emphasis. "Genuinely" works if the context has led us to think something might not be genuine, but, again, not as a prop. One way to test it is by writing your sentence with it in place, then taking it out, and seeing if the sentence works better. It usually will, because "genuinely", like "to be honest", can easily backfire, saying more about your credibility than about your subject.

Be playful

Handle this one with care: there is a time for play and it's probably not in the middle of an exam, still less a personal statement. But play is a bigger thing than it may appear in the rear-view mirror. "Children learn through play," Brian Eno said in his John Peel Lecture for the BBC in 2015. "Adults play through art." And there's so much fun to be had in playing with words. Take this poem by Brian Bilston, who has been called the Banksy of Twitter. He may be only a figment of his own imagination, but he makes thousands of people smile. While most of his poems are light entertainment, this one, posted in 2016, is playful to the point of being deadly serious.

REFUGEES

They have no need of our help
So do not tell me
These haggard faces could belong to you or me
Should life have dealt a different hand
We need to see them for who they really are
Chancers and scroungers
Layabouts and loungers
With bombs up their sleeves
Cut-throats and thieves
They are not
Welcome here
We should make them
Go back to where they came from
They cannot
Share our food
Share our homes
Share our countries
Instead let us
Build a wall to keep them out
It is not okay to say
These are people just like us
A place should only belong to those who are born there
Do not be so stupid to think that
The world can be looked at another way

(now read from bottom to top)

This poem isn't complicated, nor is it word-perfect (the second-last line is missing an "as"). It's not even all that poetic. But it makes one point so strongly that it stays with you. Last time I looked, it had been re-tweeted 16,000 times, and by 2018 there were plans to turn it into a children's book.

REPETITION OR VARIATION?

One of the redeeming features of illness is that you can't infect yourself – that nasty cold of yours can't give you another cold. One of the tricky things about writing is that you can infect yourself. We're inclined to use a word or phrase or construction, then use it again five minutes later – and what was five minutes for us may be five seconds for the reader.

Repetition isn't always bad: there are some famous lines that run on it. "To be or not to be: that is the question." "The name's Bond – James Bond." "Never apologise, never explain" (terrible advice, handsomely expressed). Repetition is powerful, but perilous – it can easily bore or bug the reader, it can be distracting or jarring, especially if it's accidental (and we can usually tell). But sometimes variation is worse, especially if it means blindly replacing a name with a description. You're reading a story about Adele and she suddenly becomes "the 30-year-old", "the millionaire singer" and then "the *Skyfall* star", none of which feels natural, and one of which is surely Daniel Craig. The best option may well be the simplest one, "she" or "her", which will mean you have to rejig the sentence. Repetition is often a side-effect of structure.

Sometimes the problem lies not with the second use of a word, but the first. "J.L. Carr's masterpiece *A Month in the Country* only runs to 85 pages," said Standpoint magazine in May 2016. "If only more writers realised that length isn't everything." It's a shrewd point, crisply phrased, apart from that repeat of "only", which is a clodhopper. The second "only" is needed, because "if only" is an idiom meaning "I wish that", but the first "only" isn't, and it's easily replaced: you could say "*A Month in the Country* runs to just 85 pages" or "*A Month in the Country* runs to a mere 85 pages". There are about 180,000 English words in current use, according to the Oxford English Dictionary, and quite a few of them are able stand-ins for each other.

SURPRISING THE READER

In *Such, Such Were the Joys* (1952), George Orwell writes about something he felt as a small boy:

> Love, the spontaneous, unqualifed emotion of love, was something I could only feel for people who were young. Towards people who were old ... I could feel reverence, respect, admiration or compunction, but I seemed cut off from them by a veil of fear and shyness mixed up with physical distaste. People are too ready to forget the child's physical shrinking from the adult. The enormous size of grown-ups, their ungainly, rigid bodies, their coarse wrinkled skins, their great relaxed eyelids, their yellow teeth, and the whiffs of musty clothes and beer and sweat and tobacco that disengage from them at every movement!

Orwell believed that writing should be clear and vigorous, and this passage is both. In *Strictly English* (2010) Simon Heffer salutes its "astonishing clarity". Orwell has worked out what he wants to say and says it with passion and precision, showing us some things ("cut off by a veil") and telling us others ("fear and shyness ... physical distaste"). He uses his senses, capturing smells and sights: the grown-ups have "rigid bodies", "coarse wrinkled skins", four different whiffs, and, best of all, "great relaxed eyelids". Being relaxed is usually a happy state, and "great", too, tends to be a good thing, but Orwell remembers how big and droopy those eyelids seemed to him, and finds words to say so that turn two pluses into a minus – in a good way.

YOUR TURN

Here is a clumsy sentence quoted in *The Penguin Writer's Manual* (2002).

> *One of the most attractive things about South Africa is the fact that it has such a variety of different scenery.*

Try reading it aloud. As the authors of the manual say, it has a "kind of stutter" in the middle, because of all the short words in a row. Can you rewrite it to make it run more smoothly? (See page 106)

IT'S BEFORE
EXCEPT AFTER

Chapter 4

KNOW THE BASICS

Tennis players have to know the difference between a serve and a volley, and practise both – even if they're among the best in the world. Writing is much the same. The fundamental things apply, and you need a firm grasp of them. Looking at other books on writing, I found that they were apt to get bogged down in the finer points of grammar, so this book is just going to give you the basics. They are rough and ready, and leave out some of the many exceptions to the rules, but they will stand you in good stead 95 times out of 100.

All the grammar you need

Remember your teacher long ago talking about the parts of speech? If you didn't take it in then, now is the time to nail it. For the full story, you need a grammar book (the most entertaining is *For Who The Bell Tolls* by David Marsh, 2013); this is just a rough guide, designed to get you through most situations.

A part of speech is just a category of words that do much the same job.

Parts of speech

There are four big ones...

a noun	a thing – one you can see or touch **(chair, bus, cake)** or one you can't **(peace, love, understanding).** The ones you can't see or touch are abstract nouns. The ones with capital letters **(Paris, Facebook, Beyonce)** are proper nouns
a verb	a doing word – **go, see, live, love, laugh**
an adjective	a word that describes a noun – **good, bad, hot, cold, super califragilisticexpialidocious**
an adverb	the same, but for verbs – **well, badly, hotly, coldly**

... Four little ones ...

a pronoun	a little word that saves us having to use names all the time – **I, you, he, she, it, we, they**
a preposition	a little word that tells you where things are – **in, on, up, down, to, from.** Or modifies the meaning of a verb: **to piss** is not the same thing as to **piss off**
a conjunction	a little or medium-sized word that joins two thoughts – **and, but, if, though**
an exclamation	a little word that expresses a greeting or response, like an emoticon – **yes, no, wow, hey, OMG, d'oh**, and many swearwords

… And a few minor ones

a number you've known what they are since you were about **three**

an article a little word that goes before a noun – **the, a, an**. Some languages don't bother with them

a determiner a little word that distinguishes one thing from another – **this, that, either, both**

a gerund a noun made out of a verb – **seeing** is **believing.** Latin gerunds end in -ndum, and some of them live on as English words: **referendum, memorandum, addendum**

Tenses: the three basic ones…

the present I love you.

the past I loved you once.

the future I will always love you.

The three continuous ones…

the continuous present something happening now, but not only at this moment: **I am studying Arabic.** In questions, we use it a lot: **What are you doing?**

the present perfect something that began in the past and hasn't stopped: **I've loved you for a long, long time.**

the imperfect something in the past that carried on for a while: **When the earthquake began, I was eating my lunch.**

… And the two uncommon ones

the pluperfect needed when you're already in the past and want to go back further: **She had loved him once.**

the future perfect needed when you're in the future and want to go back a bit: **By 2020, they will have been together for 30 years.**

Verbs are like people: they have moods

There are six main ones...

The indicative — the one you don't have to think about, because most verbs are in it, including both the verbs in this sentence. It's "the mood ... used for ordinary objective statements, questions, etc" (Dictionary.com)

The imperative — telling someone to do something: **Go – walk out the door.**

The subjunctive — showing "what is imagined or wished or possible" (OxfordDictionaries.com).
Can be hard to spot as it often resembles the past tense.
As Ralph Fiennes says, over and over again, in Hail Caesar! (2016): **Would that it were so simple.**

The conditional — may or might, mainly: **You may come with me; I might even enjoy it.**

The infinitive — the purest form of the verb, with **to** in front of it, to denote its essence: **To err is human, to forgive divine.**

The interrogative — for questions: **Do you love him?** It goes last here, partly because some experts question whether it counts as a separate mood, and partly to make sure this quick guide has gone to the infinitive and beyond.

Punctuation on a plate: the bread and butter...

Full stop — a pause between sentences:
The cat sat on the mat. Then it saw a mouse.

Comma — a shorter pause in mid-sentence:
The cat sat on the mat, until it saw a mouse.
In pairs, a way to park a description or a name:
The cat, which was fast becoming an internet sensation, sat on the mat.
The England manager, Sam Allardyce, has picked his first squad.
Sometimes people see the need for the first comma, only to blow it with the second.
After the Brexit vote, a blue plaque was stuck on Boris

Johnson's house in London. It said: "BOJO, destroyer of cosmopolitan unity and passer of buck lives here".

Apostrophe (i) to show that a final S is possessive, not plural: *I love Bart's hair in The Simpsons.*
(ii) to stand in for a missing letter in a contraction: *don't, won't, wasn't, it's* (which is always short for *it is* or *it has*)

Hyphen to show that two words are parcelled up as one part of speech: *the full-time whistle*
(it's not a full whistle, or a time whistle: it only makes sense as a full-time whistle).
Also needed when a noun and a preposition team up to form a noun:
I left my passport at check-in.
– but not when the same noun and preposition team up to form a verb:
You need your passport to check in.

Question mark to show that you're asking a question. *Got it?*

Exclamation mark to show that you're exclaiming. *Got it!* (Try not to use it for jokes. "Five exclamation marks, the sure sign of an insane mind" – Terry Pratchett)

Quote marks to show that the words are someone else's, or yours in the past.
"You're fired," said Lord Sugar.
"You're joking," I replied.

… And the jam

Colon to show that one point leads on to the next.
The past is a foreign country: they do things differently there.
Or to introduce a list. *England squad: Cook (captain), Hales, Root…*

Semi-colon to show that two points exist in parallel. *Some people specialise; others juggle.*
Or to separate items on a list, when some of them include a comma:
Also on the bill are Damon Albarn, with the Orchestra of Syrian Musicians; the Last Shadow Puppets, featuring Alex Turner from the Arctic Monkeys; and the Labour leader, Jeremy Corbyn.

Dash on its own, for when the train of thought takes a sudden turn.
The cat sat on the mat – the mouse mat.

in pairs: a way of parking one thought inside another. *The cat – true to form – sat on the mat.*

Brackets to show that your point is an aside. (Brackets are always found in pairs. If a sentence begins inside them, it ends inside them too.)

Ellipsis three dots, showing that you've left some words out of a quote, or that your point is knowingly unfinished, or you want it to hover in the air...

Quote marks are for quoting

Nervous writers tend to use a lot of quote marks, as if unaware that there's a good way of using them and a bad way. The good way is, as the name suggests, for quoting. Any time you use somebody's exact words, quote marks are needed; they are a graceful acknowledgement (these words aren't mine) which can also be a useful get-out (I didn't say this, Donald Trump did). The bad way is when you're not quoting anyone, just trying to handle a word with rubber gloves. "The great sweep of economic history," Bloomberg Businessweek argued after the Brexit vote, "is a series of 'rises' and 'falls' — from the fall of Rome to the rise of China." The second rise, and the second fall, are the right ones – no quote marks required.

If in doubt

Keep it simple. Full stops are your friend, and so are commas. Colons and semi-colons are good cards to play as long as you know the difference between them. If not, they leave you trying hard to appear clever, which is never a good look. And even when you get them right, they are best used sparingly – if one sentence has a colon or semi-colon, let the next one flow.

Commas between adjectives

When using two or three adjectives together, most people separate them with a comma or a conjunction. "The stranger was tall, dark and handsome." If you favour a second comma there, after "dark", you're a believer in the Oxford comma, which is fine as long as you're consistent about it.

Sometimes you can just run one adjective after the other to quicken the pace: "It was a bright cold day in April," Orwell begins Nineteen Eighty Four, "and the clocks were striking thirteen." Philip Pullman takes this a step further and turns it into a party trick: "She laid it on the table, and she sensed John Faa's massive simple curiosity and Farder Coram's bright flickering intelligence both trained on it like searchlights."

Comma of the century, so far

If there was an award for the best piece of punctuation – and there surely should be – the mantelpiece at Lin-Manuel Miranda's place in New York would be even more congested than it already is. Of all the bright ideas in his masterpiece, *Hamilton*, the deftest may be the comma that occurs when the main character is writing to his sister-in-law. "My dearest, Angelica," he begins. She doesn't return the comma ("My dearest Alexander"), but she does pick him up on it:

> In a letter I received from you two weeks ago
> I noticed a comma in the middle of a phrase.
> It changed the meaning. Did you intend this?
> One stroke and you've consumed my waking days.

Hamilton doesn't answer, except to acknowledge the comma's presence. He doesn't have to, as we sense that it wouldn't be there if it wasn't loaded with meaning. On Twitter, the suspicion is confirmed:

> **Lin-Manuel Miranda** @Lin_Manuel
>
> And if you think it's easy to convey the notion of comma sexting in a lyric, you are mistaken. That sh*t took WEEKS.

Syntax without tears

Clauses

A clause is a group of words that contains a subject and a verb. The cat doesn't have to sit on the mat to make a clause – it just has to do something. "The cat yawned": that's enough.

Clauses are like people on motorbikes: they're either in the driving seat or the sidecar – they're either a main clause or a subordinate clause. "The cat yawned" is a main clause. "When the cat yawned" is a subordinate clause. It needs a main clause with it to make a complete sentence: "When the cat yawned, the dog barked."

Relative clauses – the ones which begin with "who" or "which" or "whom" or "whose" or occasionally "that", and are not questions – are always subordinate. "The cat, which had got the cream, sat on the mat."

Phrases

A phrase is a small group of words that come together to form a unit but not a clause. "On the mat" is a phrase. "The cat sat" is not, because it contains a main verb.

Word order

A lot of the time it's straightforward – just follow your instinct. "The cat has got the cream." Nobody would put those words in any other order, unless they were Yoda or a particularly desperate songwriter.

English has no trouble with the basic trio of subject-verb-object, but when they are joined by an adverb, things get complicated. "I will be with you, whatever. But this is the moment to assess bluntly the difficulties." – Tony Blair, memo to George W Bush, 2002, disclosed in the Chilcot Report, 6 July 2016. The first of these sentences has already gone down in history as a blank cheque for which hundreds of thousands of people paid with their lives. But it's the second, the more sensible of the two, that gets into a tangle. Blair put "bluntly" in an odd place, probably because he was straining to avoid a split infinitive ("to bluntly assess"). The best way out might have been to stick with the same words and tweak the syntax: "But this is the moment to be blunt in assessing the difficulties."

Front-loading

Many an excellent sentence has a bit that comes before the subject. But so do some bad ones, because the writer forgets that the bit at the front applies to the whole sentence. "In 2005 she founded a karaoke club business, two years later joined the board of Marks & Spencer, and has just become a non-executive director of Twitter" – The Times on Martha Lane Fox, 9 May 2016. "In 2005" applies to the whole shebang, so it contradicts "two years later" and "has just". It's a problem that is easily fixed. You just need to add another "she" after "two years later", and a third before "has just". Little words are like insects: they do more for us than we might think.

RULES WORTH OBEYING

Don't split the infinitive

Of all the bees in the stickler's bonnet, this may be the one with the loudest buzz. For some reason, perhaps because the infinitive has a certain purity to it, the idea arose at some point that you shouldn't park an adverb, or anything else, between the "to" and the verb.

There are ways round it. You can rephrase, as with the Tony Blair quote on page 45, or see if the adverb can be cut. The Football Association has a mission statement which includes this line: "England teams aim to intelligently dominate possession selecting the right moments to progress the play and penetrate the opposition." As sentences go, this is like England's performance against Iceland in 2016: so bad you hardly know where to begin. But one phrase stands out like a corner taken by Harry Kane – "to intelligently dominate". It's weird (in football, any form of domination will do fine), it's clearly written by a committee, and it's a split infinitive. Next time that committee meets, its members either need to ditch the claim to intelligence, or detach it from their dreams of domination.

Do bother with "whom"

"Those whom the gods love die young," the saying goes. But it seems that the gods are not great fans of "whom", which has lived to a great age and has been dying a slow and painful death for decades. To the traditionalist, "whom" is needed whenever the relative pronoun is not the subject of the verb, so you have "Romeo, who loves Juliet", or "Romeo, whom Juliet loves". To the modernist, "whom" feels stiff and starchy, and isn't needed, because the word order tells us who is loving who(m). The traditionalist retorts that we still use "him", which is another example of a Saxon accusative, as are "her", "me", "us" and "them", all of them going strong. The modernist notes that "you" doesn't have an accusative and we don't miss it. The person who can see both sides stifles a yawn and wonders if we can move on.

My feeling is that it is still, just, worth bothering with "whom", but only if you can use it with confidence. If not, you may need to do a little homework on the difference between subjects and objects. If you're still not confident after that, stick with "who" for the moment. This is what Wayne Rooney does. "Sir Alex was really clever like that," he told the Daily Mail in August 2016. "He knew who he could have a go at, who it was best to leave alone." To anyone but a stickler, that is a perfectly decent sentence: even if Rooney had written it in an exam, he wouldn't have been marked down.

RULES WORTH BREAKING

Don't start a sentence with And or But

This is just nonsense. The King James Bible, one of the most stylish books ever written, starts thousands of sentences with "And". You can begin a title with it: "And I Love Her" is one of the Beatles' best-loved album tracks. And it can even be the first word of a whole piece. William Blake's poem 'Jerusalem', now better known as a majestic hymn, begins: "And did those feet in ancient time ..."

Don't end a sentence with a preposition

"She looked at me closely; she was nice to be looked at by." – Julian Barnes, *Metroland* (1980). That line hits the spot because it feels new and rings true. The sentence ends with not one preposition but two. Barnes is a precise stylist who, not long before he wrote that, had been working as a lexicographer on the Oxford English Dictionary (he had the rare honour of writing the entry on "fuck"). So he would have known that he was breaking a rule, and he was right to, because it's an odd rule, more a matter of taste than anything else, and poorly suited to English, with its abundance of verbs that end in a preposition – just look at the differences between "look at", "look out", "look into", "look over", "look up" and "look back".This rule was famously mocked by Winston Churchill, rounding on an editor who cited it: "This is arrant pedantry, up with which I will not put." The story may be apocryphal, but the point is valid – all the more so as time goes on, and writing, inch by inch, falls out of love with formality.

NOT ALL MISTAKES ARE EQUAL

Mistakes are like taxes: they sit on a sliding scale. The worst are the ones that change your meaning (leaving out "not", or typing "now" instead). The next worst are the ones that make your meaning ambiguous. Then come the ones that make you look stupid, which include some of the most common spelling mistakes ("embarassment", "seperate" – see page 51). Fourth come the tiny typos that make you look careless:

> **Uni of Leicester** @uniofleicester 5h
>
> A top 1% world university & Britian's most affordable university. Study with us this September. Open Day 22 July.

And last come the changes made by your auto-correct, which also make you look careless, but at least come with half an excuse. It wasn't me – it was my phone.

SEVEN BAD WORDS

Genuinely	has any sentence ever been improved by adding it?
Literally	ubiquitous in conversation, perilous on the page
Substantial	full of hot air: if a footballer is said to have "substantial technical ability", it just means good technique
Considerable	sounds important, means hardly anything
Like	(meaning sort of) works in conversation, dead on the page
Very	indispensable in conversation, but a boomerang on the page – you use it to strengthen your point, only to find that it weakens it
Unsurprisingly	(a) clumsy, (b) shorthand for "skip this sentence"

EASY MISTAKES TO MAKE

Often misspelt

Embarrassment	it has to have that double R before the ass
Harassment	single R – it rhymes with embarrassment, but doesn't share the double R
Separate	not seperate because it's derived from paro in Latin – to prepare or get
Accommodation	needs the double M as well as the double C
Independent	three Es, no A; same with independence
Descendants	two Es, one A
Surprise	needs an R either side of the P (because it comes from French: sur + prise)
Liaise	needs an I either side of the A

Often mistaken for each other

You're and your	"you're" is always short for you are "your" isn't short for anything – it means "belonging to you"
Its and it's	"its" always, but always, means "of it" "it's" never means "of it": it can only be short for "it" is or "it has"
They're, their and there	"they're" is always short for "they are" "their" always means "belonging to them" "there" means "in that place"; only "there" is likely to be followed by "is"
Whose and who's	"whose" always means "of whom"

	"who's" is always short for "who is" or "who has"
Effect and affect	effect means to make something happen: *he effected his getaway* affect means to have an impact on, or to put on: *the red card definitely affected the result; she affected a French accent*
Differ and defer	to differ is to be different or to disagree; to defer is to put off
Cease and seize	to cease is to stop; to seize is to grab
Flu, flew and flue	flu, short for influenza, is a bug; flew is the past tense of fly; a flue is a duct for smoke
Imply and infer	to imply something is to hint at it; to infer is to take the hint
Led and lead	led is always the past tense of lead (which rhymes with weed); lead, which rhymes with wed, is never the past tense of lead because it's a metal
Lent and leant	lent is the past tense of lend; leant is the past tense of lean
Past and passed	the past is the time that has been and gone, and past is also a preposition meaning after ("past your bedtime"); passed is the past tense of pass: she passed her test, he passed the buck.
Lose and loose	loose is the opposite of tight; lose is the opposite of gain, win or find

Often misused

Anticipate	doesn't mean "expect" (the dictionaries have caved in on this, but the purists haven't, so you can humour them, and show some class, by using "anticipate" to mean "pre-empt")
Humbled	doesn't mean "proud"
Reticent	doesn't mean "reluctant"
Constantly	doesn't mean "occurring repeatedly": that's "continually"
Nor	means "and... not", so can't have "and" in front of it

We need to talk about... tautology

Things can't revert back to how they were, costs can't be cheap or expensive, quality can't be good. You can forward an email, or pass it on, but you can't forward it on; you can watch, or look on, but you can't watch on. Tautology is when you make the same point twice in the same sentence. Quality has excellence built in to it, so it can only be low or high. The "re-" in revert means back, so "revert back" doesn't add anything, except the suspicion that you don't know what you're talking about. Cost, like quality, can only be high or low; it's the item itself that is cheap or expensive.

"They'll be stranded alone for a month" – Bear Grylls

"We mustn't over-exaggerate" – Tim Henman, BBC 5 Live, 4 July 2016

"United Together" – slogan at Democrat National Congress, 25 July 2016

We need to talk about... idiom

Idiom, from the ancient Greek for private or individual, is a word that covers the quirks of a language – the phrases that mean something distinct from their constituent parts, the tiny rules that tell us what goes with what. "Will America's young take to [Hillary] Clinton," asked The Guardian's Washington bureau chief in July 2016, "or take to the streets?"

"Shoulders can carry glory. One thing they shouldn't have to carry is dandruff." (Head & Shoulders ad featuring footballer Joe Hart). Very true about the dandruff, but shoulders don't carry glory. Nothing does. Glory can be taken or grabbed or chased or dreamt of, but, being weightless, it has no need to be carried.

Don't make simple things complicated

"By 2010, when Cameron took power, the challenge posed by the credit crunch had already been met: the economy was growing again and the level of public debt was manageable in terms of both British-historical and contemporary cross-country comparisons." – letter from Dr William Dixon and Dr David Wilson, The Guardian, 22 July 2016. Cross-country, to most people, means a type of drive or a type of running, not a type of comparison. The two doctors could have said "manageable compared to Britain's peers and to its own past", which is shorter and clearer.

Half of writing is editing

And you've come along at the right time for it, because your screen makes crossing out easier than it has ever been.

Be consistent

Writing is like parenting: often, it's not the choice you make that matters most, but whether you stick to it. If you start a story in the present tense, stay in it unless there's a reason to switch that the story demands. If you prefer to spell judgement as judgment, that's fine by the dictionary, but you need to keep on doing it. If you use double quote marks, don't switch to single, except for a quote within a quote. If you refer to Richard III, you can call him Richard at the next mention, but you can't call him Gloucester, or Richard, Duke of Gloucester, without making it clear that this is the same person at an earlier stage. If you use "you" meaning "one", don't change to "one" in mid-stream. Better still, don't use it at all: leave it to the royal family.

The place where consistency counts the most is the singular and the plural. "Manchester police baffled," says the Manchester Evening News, "after reports of a dead animal in the canal turns out to be a duvet filled with coconuts." It sounds a cracking story, but it would be even better if the plural subject of the subordinate clause, "reports", had not been attached to the singular verb "turns out". The New Yorker, normally a paragon of polished prose, commits the same howler: "Talk of big European and American banks quitting the City of London, which by many measures is the world's largest financial hub, are exaggerated."

Many writers are lured down this path by a "one of... that" construction. "The importance of luck," says The Times, "is one of the big issues that divides conservatives from liberals." It's an error so common that it may soon cease to be an error, but it hasn't got there yet. The final clause there, starting with "that", is governed by "the big issues", not by the "one", so it should be "the big issues that divide conservatives from liberals". Otherwise, that plural is meaningless, and makes you wonder whether the writer has thought the sentence through.

Consistency helps with syntax too. Take this point, made by Peter Hyman, headmaster of School 21 in East London, to The Guardian, in May 2016: "What will be left for humans when the robots arrive? It's obvious: creative jobs, jobs that need empathy, jobs where you're generating ideas, jobs where you're problem-solving. All these are undervalued in schools." It's an excellent point, but if Hyman had had the chance to polish it, he might have turned "creative jobs" round to say "jobs that are creative", so that all four of the phrases about jobs shared the same shape. Syntax works better when you have the courage of your constructions.

YOUR WRITING'S IMPOSSIBLE TO READ – HAVE YOU CONSIDERED BECOMING A DOCTOR?

HOW TO WRITE AN ESSAY

Give reasons for every point you make

The reasons are more important than the point.

Sound from the start as if you know how you will finish

This was the main thing my tutor at university hoped to find. It may have been the only thing that got me a place.

Come up with good lines

> "Writing free verse is like playing tennis with the net down."
> **– Robert Frost**

> "There is no money in poetry, but then there is no poetry in money, either." **– Robert Graves**

> "A lie can be halfway round the world while the truth is putting on its shoes." **– Mark Twain**

One at a time

An "also" cannot be followed by another "also". A "this" shouldn't be followed by another "this" (a "this" followed by a "that" may work). A "but" shouldn't be followed by another "but" – it's like asking the reader to do two U-turns.

ESSAY PLAN
1. GET GIVEN ESSAY
2. FREAK OUT
3. PRETEND IT'S NOT HAPPENING
4. WATCH TV.
PLAY GAMES
5. REALITY CHECK
6. PANIC
7. SIT UP ALL NIGHT
8. WRITE ESSAY
9. GET B-
Newman.

25 PHRASES THAT ARE NEVER RIGHT

what people sometimes say	*what they mean*
would of, should of, could of	would have, should have, could have
each others	each other
over-exaggerate	exaggerate
the least number of	the fewest
between you and I	between you and me
myself and Barack	Barack and I (or me, if it's the object)
revert back	revert, or go back
I thought to myself	I thought, or I said to myself
up until	up to, or until
in school	at school
suited for	suited to
optimistic of	hopeful of
prefer… over	prefer… to
between… or	between… and
amount of [anything plural]	number of
less [anything plural]	fewer
under the circumstances	in the circumstances (they stand around, not above)
hone in	home in (hone means sharpen)
first-year anniversary	first anniversary (anni- means year)
to step foot	to set foot, or to step

one of the only	either the only, or one of the few
mens, womens, childrens	men's, women's, children's
the criteria is	the criteria are, or the criterion is
the right pronounciation	the right pronunciation

RARELY RIGHT

what we say	*what to replace it with, and why*
I think	nothing – it goes without saying
very	nothing – it tends to backfire, weakening your point rather than reinforcing it
utilise	use – there is never any need for management jargon
incredible, incredibly	something specific that leaves the reader sharing your incredulity
hugely	there's no adverb from big or small, because we don't often do things in a big or small way. When did you last do something in a way that was huge? If you're just in need of a word to beef up an adjective, choose a stronger one
just desserts	the perfect phrase for when you next come across some fair-minded puddings. If you mean the result the person deserved, you need "just deserts" – meaning "deserved things", an archaic noun from the same root as the verb
the former… the latter	names or pronouns – they don't send the reader back
beg the question	raise the question – "beg" takes something simple and makes it complicated

NEVER GOOD

Plagiarism if you want to use someone else's words, just quote them

Gush because writing is cooler and drier than conversation

Guff because each word has to earn its place and pull its weight

Waffle because it wastes the reader's time, and yours

Chapter 5

BE ORGANISED

When you have a job, you soon realise that half the battle is getting organised, both for work and at work. Writing is like that too.

Whether you're writing an essay or a story or a poem, you are going to need a beginning, a middle and an end. Whether you have the middle and the end mapped out at the beginning is another matter. "My advice is to write your story first," Philip Pullman told a packed theatre at the Oxford Literary Festival in 2015, "and make the plan afterwards." And he used to be an English teacher.

But you can bet that when he embarked on His Dark Materials, he had some inkling of where Lyra and Will would end up, and what would happen to the Authority. It's said that when J.K. Rowling started writing the first Harry Potter book, she knew how the whole saga would finish, but not how she would get there. A destination is essential, a plan is desirable, and some flexibility is advisable, because you may well have more ideas during the writing than you do beforehand. But it's all too easy for advice to be abstract, so here are some practical tips.

Know your priorities

Are you telling a story or making a case? If it's a story, it needs to begin and end with something happening. "The third act must build, build, build in tempo until the last event," the great film-maker Billy Wilder said, "and then… that's it. Don't hang around." If it's an argument, it can begin with an event, an anecdote, a joke, an observation or almost anything that's relevant, but it needs to end with a point. By knowing the genre of what you're writing, you hand yourself a compass. If it's a poem, it can be more intense and elusive than a story. If it's a story, it can be more free-wheeling than an essay. If it's a Facebook post, it shouldn't read like a press release. If it's any of the above, it shouldn't read like gibberish.

Separate your thoughts

There are people who will advise you not to use Wikipedia, but it has two great uses for writers. It's a mine of information, some of which is accurate; and it's a masterclass in how not to write. Take the entry on Orkney, which I stumbled on when I was referring to George Mackay Brown on page 27. "The significant wind and marine energy resources," it said, "are of growing importance." This is not a terrible sentence – in fact, by Wikipedian standards, it's close to the top of the class – but it does commit one small offence. "Significant" and "of… importance" mean more or less the same thing, so you could cut "significant" and lose hardly anything. The two ends of the sentence trip over each other, like a dancing dad, trying to place his left foot on the spot already occupied by his right.

Make internal sense

"Globalisation and migration have brought a new era of people-trafficking, with about 20 million now in forced labour," The Daily Telegraph reported in July 2016. "The problem is that the police don't recognise it when they see it, and end up prosecuting victims. Barack Obama has spoken eloquently about this, but only one politician has passed proper legislation to deal with it: Mrs May's Modern Slavery Act of 2015." This is good writing, conversational and clear, an Orwell-style window on an appalling state of affairs, but one thing goes awry. If it says "only one politician" before the colon, then the thing that comes after it has to be Mrs May herself. It should say "Mrs May, with her Modern Slavery Act of 2015". The structure of the sentence insists on it. This internal logic makes writing easier, because it reduces our options. That last part of the sentence should have been the easiest to write, and perhaps it was – the error may have crept in at the editing stage.

Hold on to your rabbit

> "There is always a well-known solution to every human problem — neat, plausible, and wrong." – **H.L. Mencken, 1920**

> "At school they taught me how to be So pure in thought and word and deed. They didn't quite succeed" – **Pet Shop Boys, It's a Sin, 1987**

> Falling Awake – **Alice Oswald, 2016**

Here are three pieces of writing, from three different eras, in three different genres – an essay, a song and the title of a book of poems – and they all obey the same rule: the most important word in a sentence is the last. The writer leads you one way, then surprises you. None of the sentences is complex, all of the words apart from "plausible" are simple, yet each time the effect is satisfying. We are programmed to enjoy a twist in the tale, and for maximum impact it should be a twist in the tail, to allow the surprise to hang in the air. Alice Oswald manages to pull her rabbit out of the hat in the space of two words, delaying the surprise till the final syllable, playing off the fact that "asleep" and "awake" begin the same way. Any of us might have noticed that, but it took a poet to make something of it.

If the most important word in a sentence is the last, a few other things follow. Any dull bits need to be dispatched before you get to the end: if in doubt, park them in the middle. If a word has come at the end of one sentence, it shouldn't come at the end of the next, or it will have stolen its own thunder. In a list, the final entry should be the most engaging one. And in a paragraph, the most important sentence is the last.

Ditch the comma splice

One day in July 2016, as the political world reeled from the vote for Brexit, The Guardian ran this headline: "The country needs a diplomat, Boris Johnson is a liability". Here is an example of the dreaded comma splice: when a sentence has two main clauses with only a comma to join or separate them. There may once have been a "but" before the "Boris" which was binned to save space; if so, it came at a price that was not worth paying. There were other options, all shorter, that might have been better:

1. Keep the two main clauses, and the comma, and add a conjunction:

> "Britain needs a diplomat, but Boris Johnson is a liability"

2. Drop the second main verb so that "needs" governs both halves

of the sentence:

> "The nation needs a diplomat, not this liability"

3. Add "when" to make one of the clauses subordinate to the other:

> "When Britain needs a diplomat, it gets a liability – Boris"

If you remember only one of these options, let it be 1. Just add "but" – or, as it might be in other examples, "and". Make friends with those two: they will get you out of plenty of scrapes.

Keep your sentences short

The danger with short sentences is that your writing becomes staccato. The danger with long ones is that you lose the plot, and the reader. Which of these dangers is the greater? Ideally, you'll mix up the lengths of your sentences, but if in doubt, lean towards the short side. One of the most successful long-form stories of the past decade was a piece by Michael Pollan for the New York Times Magazine on the western world's messed-up relationship with food. Even though it ran to 10,000 words, it became the most read feature on nytimes.com that year, partly on the strength of a memorable opening: "Eat food. Not too much. Mainly plants."

Samuel Beckett once took the same idea even further: "Ever tried. Ever failed. No matter. Try again. Fail again. Fail better."

Contrast those two with this, from a leading economist: "... the easy presumption of the last two decades of the 20th century that the listed company should not only be the dominant form of economic organisation of medium and large enterprises but the only form of economic organisation appropriate for such enterprises was a mistake. Too often conversion to a listed public company was the result of a greedy generation's anxiety to realise the goodwill

Samuel Beckett: "Try again. Fail again. Fail better."

created over a long history for the benefit of those who had the good fortune to be around at the time" – John Kay. Try reading that aloud and you'll be gasping for breath. A respected thinker, and a writer with plenty of crisp words in his locker (easy, greedy, goodwill, fortune), Kay is so busy thinking here that even the good words end up as croutons, drowning in a goulash of guff.

Hit the return key

Like "and" and "but", paragraphs are your friend. As well as giving the reader a break, they make your thinking clearer and radiate confidence. For some reason, though, this is a card we are often reluctant to play. When writing by hand, we can get sucked into putting down one thing after another, and only realise too late that there was a natural break half way through. When writing on a screen, we can do something about it, so that's the time to get into the habit of making your paragraphs shorter.

As a rule of thumb, **you need a new paragraph for each cluster**

of thoughts. If it threatens to get too big, you can split it in two, or three. If you're writing dialogue, you can do what novelists do and start a new paragraph for every new speaker, which makes it a lot clearer who is saying what.

If you're introducing a new point, a new piece of evidence or a new idea, reach for the return key. Do it where it seems logical to give the reader a pause for breath. Try to vary the length of your paragraphs, just as you do with your sentences. Rhythm is almost as important in prose as it is in poetry.

There's a paragraph from a classic comic novel, Evelyn Waugh's *Decline and Fall* (1928), which the publisher of this book, Jon Connell, particularly likes. It shows a Welsh band arriving at a school sports day, as seen by a character called Dr Fagan.

> Ten men of revolting appearance were approaching from the drive. They were low of brow, crafty of eye, and crooked of limb. They advanced huddled together with the loping tread of wolves, peering about them furtively as they came, as though in constant terror of ambush; they slavered at their mouths, which hung loosely over the receding chins, while each clutched under his ape-like arm a burden of curious and unaccountable shape. On seeing the Doctor they halted and edged back, those behind squinting and moulting over their companions' shoulders.

Over to Jon. "A short sentence sets the scene, telling us what happened," he says. "A second short sentence reinforces the first, the sing-song rhythm ('low of brow, crafty of eye') ramming home how ridiculous the musicians seem. Then comes a third, much longer sentence, expanding on the second. The paragraph ends with another shortish sentence which rounds off the picture, telling us what happens when the musicians spot the doctor. (And if you think it's all a bit unfair on Welsh rustics, you're right, but that's comedy for you. Waugh's description of the posh, English Bollinger Club is just as savage.)

"Note how Waugh sticks to the same grammatical subject: the 'ten men of revolting appearance' keep reappearing as 'they'. It's like showing a scene in a film from a single camera angle. It helps us to keep things steady in our minds. In lesser hands the string of *they*s might be too repetitive, but with Waugh's sparkling imagery, varied sentence lengths, and varied word order – making sure that *they* isn't the first word in every sentence – we barely notice."

Beware of the dangler

A sign near a London station advertises the services of a personal trainer. It says: "After sitting on my arse for years, Wayne made me fighting fit again." This is a particularly fine example of the syntactical howler known as the dangling participle, or the dangler. A participle is a form of a verb that is used as an adjective ("Gone Girl", "Breaking Bad", "the smoking gun"). If a participle, or any other modifier, comes at the start of a sentence, the subject has to be the person to whom it applies. So if you start off with "After sitting on my arse for years", the subject can only be "I". Common sense may well tell us what the writer of the advert meant, but it's better to mean what you say.

BETTER LATE THAN NEVER!
RIP
Thank you

A BETTER THANK YOU LETTER

1. Don't see it as a chore. See it as a chance to show your enthusiasm, practise your writing and come up with a memorable line or two.

2. Be specific. Say things you couldn't have said beforehand – not just "thank you for the voucher, it was very generous".

3. Think about what the giver of the present or the party put into it, whether it's the thought or the time spent clearing up afterwards. Broaden out the gratitude if you can, but keep it real: don't gush or perjure yourself.

4. Say something only you can say. Tell the recipient something they don't know – the music you spent the voucher on, the person you had a good chat with at the party, the thing on the menu that was delicious, the song that got you dancing.

5. Don't worry if it's late: this is a clear case of better late than never. Writing a thank-you letter may still not be your idea of fun, but the only alternative is not writing one, which is an easy way to look ungrateful and entitled. But don't go on a guilt trip – we've all done it.

I JUST DON'T WANT TO DISCOURAGE HIM FROM WRITING
POLICE R SCUM
MUFC

Chapter 6

READ LIKE A WRITER

"'A reader lives a thousand lives before he dies,' said Jojen. 'The man who never reads lives only one.'" – George RR Martin, *A Dance with Dragons* (2011).

Of all the countless lines he has written, that is Martin's favourite. It is the story of his own life. "When I was a kid," he told an audience at the Edinburgh International Book Festival in 2014, "my world was five streets long." He lived in a dockside town in New Jersey, where his father worked as a longshoreman. "I never got away, except in books. I lived a thousand lives through books."

Writers need to be open, to words as well as the rest of the world. They don't just read books, they read newspapers. And they don't choose a newspaper for its politics, because that would be like going into the polling booth and voting for the candidate who's the best writer.

Reading doesn't just expand your world: it broadens your mind and sharpens your pencil. By writing, you will learn things the hard way, which is often the best way; but by reading, you can do it the easy way too. You can learn from other people's mistakes, and from their successes, and from everything in between.

You will see how simple a good line can be. "The past is never dead," William Faulkner wrote in *Requiem for a Nun* (1951). "It isn't even past." This was quoted by Barack Obama at a vital moment on his way to the White House in 2008, when he went against the wishes of his advisors and made a speech about race relations. He didn't quite get the quotation right, saying "the past is never dead and buried". But it was still Faulkner's line, and the fact that it played a part on the world's biggest stage, 57 years after it was published, triumphantly proved its point.

Writers read the ways other people do, for pleasure or escape, to acquire knowledge or to make sense of the human predicament. "The best moments in reading," Alan Bennett says in *The History Boys*, "are when you come across something – a thought, a feeling, a way of looking at things – which you had thought special and particular to you. Now here it is, set down by someone else, a person you have never met, someone even who is long dead. And it is as if a hand has come out and taken yours." That pleasure is waiting for us whether we write or not. But writers also read in another way, paying extra attention. A sportsman has to watch the ball, a driver has to watch the road, and a writer has to watch each word.

Writers think about the choices the author makes, the forms she uses, the things she leaves out, the fork she didn't take. They think about tone of voice; they may even read a writer for tone alone. Nobody in the 21st century needs to know anything about what lovable buffoons, omniscient valets and domineering aunts might have got up to in 1920s England, but PG Wodehouse is still read and revered by the writers' union, because they can open a book of his at random and find a sentence like this, from *Very Good, Jeeves!*

(1930): "In one second, without any previous training or upbringing, he had become the wettest man in Worcestershire."

Writers re-read, sometimes again and again, so that the plot looms less large and the technique stands out. Writers read with their ears as well as their brains, hearing the lines in their head, letting them ring out, seeing which ones resound and which fall flat. Writers look and listen hard enough to separate the strengths from the weaknesses, even in writers they admire. There are many good reasons to applaud J.K. Rowling: her plotting (seven books of twists and turns), her ingenuity (the sorting hat, the moving portraits), her characterisation (Hagrid, Dumbledore, the Weasleys), her powers of realisation (the Dementors), her good humour (Bertie Bott's Every Flavour Beans), her decency and dignity in the face of fame. But that doesn't mean you have to admire the way she uses adverbs.

> Professor McGonagall sniffed angrily.
>
> 'Oh yes, everyone's celebrating, all right,' she said impatiently...
>
> 'You can't blame them,' said Dumbledore gently. 'We've had precious little to celebrate for eleven years.'
>
> 'I know that,' said Professor McGonagall irritably.
>
> – *Harry Potter and the Philosopher's Stone* (1997)

Angrily, impatiently, gently, irritably: three of those four could have gone without saying. They are props that are not needed if the dialogue is half-decent, which it is. And, to make matters worse, they all end up in a conspicuous place, at the end of their sentence (he added tetchily).

YOU NEED TO BE MORE CONCISE
Newman.

Chapter 7

WRITE LIKE A WRITER

In June 2016 the people of Britain astonished themselves by voting to leave the European Union. A week later, the Financial Times had two columnists writing about how this fateful moment had gone for them. Here's a paragraph from each.

> "I was quite confident during the day that Remain would win, reinforced by the late opinion polls. However, results from Newcastle and Sunderland sharply changed my mood as I departed for bed, and by 6am it was all over – Brexit had triumphed." – **John Lee.**

> "All good dramas involve the suspension of disbelief. So it was with Brexit. I went to bed at 4am on Friday depressed that Britain had voted to leave the EU. The following day my gloom only deepened. But then, belatedly, I realised that I have seen this film before. I know how it ends. And it does not end with the UK leaving Europe." – **Gideon Rachman.**

The two paragraphs have plenty in common: both mention bed, both pinpoint a time of day, both express disappointment and both use the first person liberally. But only one of them reads like the work of a writer.

In John Lee's paragraph, something goes mildly awry in every line. When he says "quite confident", it's not clear if he is using "quite" in the British sense, to mean "fairly", or the American one, to mean "thoroughly". When he tacks on "reinforced" at the end of a clause in which the subject was "I", he is saying that he, not his confidence, was reinforced by the polls, which isn't the way "reinforce" works; he'd be better off with "fortified". He then reaches for "however", which, as so often, is clunky and unnatural – a sledgehammer being used to crack a "but". My guess is that he wanted to say "but", only to hear the voice of a long-dead schoolteacher in his head, saying you shouldn't begin a sentence with a conjunction.

And what did the referendum results do to his mood? They "sharply changed" it. This isn't writing, it's Russian athletics coaching: an attempt to take an ordinary verb and put it on steroids. The attempt backfires because the wording still feels weak. If you want to strengthen a verb, replace it with a stronger one. The thesaurus has plenty to offer: "transform", "darken", "sour", "ruin".

Worst of all, the paragraph finishes by saying that Brexit had triumphed, thereby telling FT readers something every last one of them already knew. There can be a place for something the reader already knows, but that place is not the end of a paragraph, or even the end of a sentence. It turns a dive into a belly flop.

Rachman's way of saying much the same thing is bolder and sharper. He opens with a big pronouncement: "All good dramas involve the suspension of disbelief." It's a generalisation, and thus potentially dodgy – if the reader can think of one good drama that doesn't involve the suspension of disbelief, Rachman will have put some of his own credibility in the toaster. But he gets away with it, partly because he moves on so fast.

It's not the only thing he gets away with. In the middle of his paragraph are two or three bum notes. "Depressed" might not be what he meant, as it's usually applied to a mood that is prolonged; he might have been better off with one of its neighbours – "dismayed", "disheartened" "downcast" or "dejected". (When he returns to his mood, he makes a better choice – "gloom".) He too places the result at the end of a sentence, thus committing a less heinous version of one of Lee's crimes. He picks up on "4am on Friday" with "the following day", which is a bit jarring (once you've gone specific, stay specific) and confusing: does he mean later on Friday, or Saturday? But his rhythm is impeccable, with its short brisk sentences, and it carries us along to the part of the paragraph that matters most – the end.

He's been talking about drama, and he has a twist of his own: Brexit is not going to happen after all. It's a rabbit produced from a hat, the opposite of Lee's floppy ending. It is proper writing. This isn't to dismiss Lee, whose column exists to give advice on personal investment; the advice is more important than the wording. In a perfect world he'd be serving up both, but it's not essential. Rachman, as one of the FT's star commentators, needs to write like a writer – and does.

Here are a few more leaves you can take out of the professionals' book.

Be curious

Ask questions, or just listen. Some writers are good talkers, but more of them are good listeners. For non-fiction, they need information and ideas; for fiction, ideas and feelings, and sometimes information too; for both, a feel for human nature.

To write, you will need to have things to say. To have things to say, you will need to listen, to absorb, to learn from people who have seen and done interesting things. If you're stuck next to an older person, you could ask what life was like for them at your age: something they say will surprise you.

Just write

It doesn't have to be for publication – better not, to begin with. You could keep a diary, not religiously, not daily, but every now and again. Write the way you take photographs, to capture something interesting. Write the way you talk about your feelings, to release something. Or not: it doesn't have to be your innermost thoughts – you could be the kind of writer that looks outwards and slips more easily into the third person than the first. If a diary seems too daunting, just take notes on a journey, a project, a new job or phase. One way or another, get into the habit of getting some words down.

And rewrite

Write something, leave it to cool, come back a few days later. It will strike you differently; you will see things you can improve. It may be in need of a polish, a trim, a full rethink, or nothing at all. Half of writing is rewriting: unlike in conversation, you are free to get it wrong first time, and that freedom is one that every writer uses.

Don't write with just your brain

Write with your eyes, your ears, your heart – more of those things if it's fiction, more brain if it's something analytical. But make sure the heart still plays a part.

Develop a voice

You already have a voice in the literal sense (the ability to talk) and you probably have one in the literary sense too (a distinctive way of talking). But the first thing to do here, as in many situations, is to steer away from the rocks of self-consciousness.

It's easier to make out someone else's voice than your own. Picture a friend or family member talking to you: what are their favourite words, their characteristic tone, the rhythms of their speech? These are the ingredients that make a voice. Before we're even aware of it, we have a distinctive voice – in fact two, one for writing and one for speaking. The two voices are siblings, perhaps even twins, but not identical. When writing, we make certain adjustments – no ums and ers, no swearing (unless it's strictly necessary, which probably means you're either writing dialogue or quoting), a wider vocabulary, some longer sentences. But we shouldn't take this too far. Some of the worst writing comes along when the writer is under the impression that writing is a different language, and starts replacing perfectly good, clear, direct words with stilted ones – "begin" becomes "commence", "also" becomes "in addition", "a lot" becomes "a substantial amount", "shown" becomes "evidenced", and the reader smells waffle or, worse, bullshit.

All this may take a long time. Paul Greengrass, the director of three of the Bourne films, started out as a maker of thoughtful documentaries and was nearly 50 when he made his first action movie. He soon became revered for his distinctive style – relentless drama, hand-held cameras, a hot-line to the viewer's nervous system. Now, when Greengrass talks to film students, he says this: "Find the song that only you can sing."

WE NEED TO TALK ABOUT...WRITER'S BLOCK

Every writer, professional or otherwise, knows how it feels to find the words refusing to flow. Here's one way of getting round it.

1. Don't panic
2. Ask yourself what has to be in there, however simple
3. Start making a list of these things
4. As you make it, think about what order the things should go in
5. Congratulate yourself – you've started writing

Be original

Originality sounds like a high bar, but it begins with a single thought. "You put together two things that have not been put together before. And the world is changed..." – Julian Barnes, *Levels of Life* (2013).

Be subtle

Life is full of fine distinctions, and writing needs to be subtle to reflect it. Better still if it's subtle and still simple. "I don't believe in God," Julian Barnes once said, "but I miss him."

Put different flavours together

As you get older, bitter chocolate is better chocolate. And so it is with writing: hundreds of great love songs are bittersweet. Here's Tom Stoppard being entertaining and erudite at the same time, and liking the effect so much that he uses it as his opening:

> *Precocious teenager, about 200 years ago, to her tutor:*
> Septimus, what is carnal embrace?
> *Tutor, suddenly spotting her mother:*
> It is the practice of throwing one's arms around a side of beef.
> – *Arcadia* (1993)

Express yourself

"When I write I am trying to express my way of being in the world. This is primarily a process of elimination: once you have removed all the dead language, the second-hand dogma, the truths that are not your own but other people's, the mottos, the slogans, the out-and-out lies of your nation, the myths of your historical moment – once you have removed all that warps experience into a shape you do not recognise and do not believe in – what you are left with is something approximating the truth of your own conception." – Zadie Smith, "Fail Better" (2007)

Don't wait for inspiration

Inspiration does exist – there are few things better than a bright idea that pops into your head, apparently unprompted. But it seldom plays more than a cameo role. The lead goes to something more earthbound: concentration, application, determination. And those, you can control.

Don't fall for the first word that comes along

"Brilliant" is another word that is becoming too weary to do its job. It's supposed to mean "shining brightly", but is now trotted out so often, in British English at any rate, that it has come to mean just "very good". If that's what you mean, you're better off with "outstanding"; if you want to keep the element of sheen, try "sparkling" or "radiant" or "scintillating".

Hold what you've just said in your head

Early in 2016, a pilot filed a report to the budget airline FlyDubai on a flight that had taken off from Dhaka. "During take-off from RW14 in DAC after V1 during rotation we experienced a bird strike on ENG#1," he wrote. "Heavy smell of burned bird felt in the cockpit and during climb engine vibration was experienced." Perhaps still reeling from this incident, the pilot wipes the first sentence from his memory before writing the second. He uses "during" for the third time, adding to his impressive collection of adverbial phrases – the first sentence started with five of them in a row, which may a world record. And he finishes with "experienced", which he has already used once, and which could be understood anyway: we know he is recounting an experience. This isn't to blame him at all – he may be using his second language (the smell was not smelt but felt), and it's not as if many of us writers can land a plane. It's just that writing, like flying, goes better when we know where we've just been.

Keep it up your sleeve

Readers love a bit of suspense. "Narrative tension," Ian McEwan has said, "is primarily about withholding information." It's a rather grey line by his high standards, but a true one.

Jane Eyre begins like this: "There was no possibility of taking a walk that day." And you instantly want to know why. Charlotte Brontë has drawn you into her web before she has even produced a character.

Mind your metaphors and similes

"A library in the middle of a community is a cross between an emergency exit, a life-raft and a festival. They are cathedrals of the mind; hospitals of the soul; theme parks of the imagination. On a cold rainy island, they are the only sheltered public spaces where you are not a consumer, but a citizen instead" – Caitlin Moran, *Moranthology* (2013). She didn't really need those semi-colons, and six metaphors on one plate may be too much. But they are good ones, fired by passion.

The point of a metaphor or simile isn't just to liken X to Y. It's to liken X to a Y that is part of the reader's world. Homer

WHATEVER HAPPENED TO HAP?

In plain English, plenty of adjectives are dead simple. Lucky is the one that goes with luck. Funny goes with fun, dirty goes with dirt, and funky goes with funk. So what does happy go with? It feels as if there ought be a noun called hap. And, to some extent, there is. We have hapless, which means much the same as luckless. We have happen, which is the verb made from the noun, like lighten or darken or hearten. It turns out that hap did exist in the late 12th century, as a Middle English word meaning either [a person's] luck or lot, or a happening. It came from Old Norse, where the word was happ. Now all we have is its ghost, animating some of the words we use most often.

compares an army to a field of corn, because every last member of his audience, listening to him sing his stories after a meal, would have known what a field of corn looked like. It's the same when Shakespeare compares a lover to a summer's day.

The distance between X and Y shouldn't be too small. No point describing cricket in terms of golf ("we were behind the eight ball").

Some are old friends, and that's fine

There are metaphors that people reach for all the time: not my cup of tea, barking up the wrong tree, plenty of fish in the sea, needle in a haystack, water under the bridge, another string to her bow. George Orwell thought we should avoid them (like the plague).

There are some words that now exist largely, or even exclusively, in metaphors – hoist by your own petard, damp squib, poisoned chalice.

If they are old friends, play around with them

One man's meat is another man's... the standard word is poison, but by now we know where you're going with it and you can substitute almost anything..

Keep your metaphors metaphorical

Some metaphors become drained of their ability to take us into a different field. "The lies of Britain's papers have been key to shaping the country's predicament," says Open Democracy. But keys don't shape anything.

There's nothing like a simile

Writers see parallels. Like this: "Persuading austerity Britain to spend billions on Trident is like convincing a tramp he needs a bazooka." – Frankie Boyle, The Guardian, 17 May 2016.

Or this: "Like a bird on the wire/ Like a drunk in a midnight choir/ I have tried, in my way, to be free" – Leonard Cohen, *Bird on the Wire* (1969).

If you're coming up with a fresh simile, as Cohen was, you probably need the "like". If you're using a familiar one, you may be better off without it. But it is never essential: "War is capitalism with the gloves off" – Tom Stoppard, *Travesties* (1974).

Find the paradox

Writers look at things sideways. Or turn them upside down and give them a shake:

> "The child is father of the man." – William Wordsworth, 'My Heart Leaps Up When I Behold' (1802).

> "Miss Brooke had that kind of beauty which seems to be thrown into relief by poor dress." – George Eliot, opening line of *Middlemarch* (1871-72).

> "And I call to you, I call to you
> But I don't call soft enough"
> – Leonard Cohen, 'Ain't No Cure for Love' (1988).

Store the bad stuff

You don't have to suffer for your art, but it helps. Anything that goes wrong in life can be stashed away, to be used as fuel for your writing. Social awkwardness? Personal turmoil? Unhappy childhood? Sorry to hear it, but it's all good material.

Revise the received wisdom

Sometimes the received wisdom is wise enough. Other times, it doesn't ring true – and as soon as you query it or vary it, you have some wisdom of your own. "The greatest lie ever told about love is that it sets you free." – Zadie Smith, *On Beauty* (2005).

Find the music in you

Words and music tend to be seen as different things, but the best words have some music in them. Toddlers know this, and so do writers. "All art," said the critic Walter Pater in 1888, "aspires to the condition of music." We write thousands of sentences that don't come close, but that shouldn't stop us trying from time to time. Listen to your sentence, even if it's never going to be read aloud. Hear the sound, the rhythm, the tempo, the timbre, the beauty. Even a string of prepositions, used as adverbs, can be musical:

> License my roving hands, and let them go
> Before, behind, between, above, below
> – John Donne, 'To His Mistress Going to Bed'

It's worth working away at a sentence till some music pops out. When the process works, it won't just be the sentence that feels better: you will have found something in yourself that you didn't know was there.

WRITING BETWEEN THE LINES

Here's a sentence by a 20th C. philosopher: "A drop of water is not immortal; it can be resolved into oxygen and hydrogen. If, therefore, a drop of water were to maintain that it had a quality of aqueousness which would survive its dissolution we should be inclined to be sceptical." – Bertrand Russell, *What I Believe* (1925).

He doesn't mention the thing he's talking about, but you get it anyway. Readers sense when they need to read between the lines, and good writers write accordingly.

YOUR TURN

1. Which of these are metaphors?

a) "All the world's a stage."

– Shakespeare, *As You Like It*

b) "I became aware of someone coughing softly by my side, like a respectful sheep trying to catch the attention of its shepherd."

– P.G. Wodehouse, *Thank You, Jeeves*

c) In Raymond Chandler's The Big Sleep, *the hero notices that the trees at a grand house were "trimmed as carefully as poodle dogs".*

d) Jeeves lugged my purple socks out of the drawer as if he were a vegetarian fishing a caterpillar out of his salad.

– P.G. Wodehouse, *My Man Jeeves*

Answers on page 106

2. Write a paragraph about a city you know, using only natural imagery.

3. "If phrases are old friends, play around with them." Here are three more sentences from Wodehouse and one by Garrison Keillor, all of which do this.

The supply of the milk of human kindness was short by several gallons.

Hell, it is well known, has no fury like a woman who wants her tea and can't get it.

I'd always thought her half-baked, but now I think they didn't even put her in the oven.

She hasn't just got a screw loose – the whole lid's blown off.

a) Give these phrases a twist so they don't feel stale.

You could have knocked me down with a feather.

It was the best thing since sliced bread.

b) Finish these sentences in the style of Wodehouse.

He was as angry as ...

She sprang out of bed like ...

4. Finish this line in the spirit of Julian Barnes (page 44)

I don't believe in private education, but...

Chapter 8

A FEW GOOD MODELS

I How to embark on an epic

The Decanter of Tokay

Lyra and her daemon moved through the darkening Hall, taking care to keep to one side, out of sight of the kitchen. The three great tables that ran the length of the Hall were laid already, the silver and the glass catching what little light there was, and the long benches were pulled out ready for the guests. Portraits of former Masters hung high up in the gloom along the walls. Lyra reached the dais and looked back at the open kitchen door and, seeing no one, stepped up beside the high table. The places here were laid with gold, not silver, and the fourteen seats were not oak benches but mahogany chairs with velvet cushions.

> *Lyra stopped beside the Master's chair and flicked the biggest glass gently with a fingernail. The sound rang clearly through the Hall.*
>
> *"You're not taking this seriously," whispered her daemon. "Behave yourself."*
>
> *Her daemon's name was Pantalaimon, and he was currently in the form of a moth, a dark brown one so as not to show up in the darkness of the Hall.*
>
> *"They're making too much noise to hear from the kitchen," Lyra whispered back. "And the Steward doesn't come in till the first bell. Stop fussing."*
>
> [Phillap Pullman, *Northern Lights*, 1995]

Philip Pullman shows us that his heroine is fearless – and so is he. He heads his first chapter "The Decanter of Tokay", happy to use not one word that may well be new to his young readers, but two. He plunges us *in medias res*, as the Romans liked to say – into the thick of things – and his first four words pick up on Rome's greatest poem. "Arms and the man…" is the way Virgil opens *The Aeneid.* "Lyra and her daemon" is an echo, a homage, and an instant incentive to read on: what's a daemon? Again, Pullman doesn't explain. He just shows us the scene, the sights and sounds of the Hall. His vocabulary is brisk and vivid: in the opening paragraph, the only words longer than two syllables are "darkening" and "mahogany". He laces his sentences with alliteration: length, laid, little light, long; hung high; flicked, fingernail. He doesn't fret about repetition, putting two "not"s in one sentence, and two "with"s with them, and using "whispered" twice in a row, where many writers would have opted for an inelegant variation. He keeps showing us the shortage of light (darkening, gloom, dark brown, darkness) and the texture of things (silver, glass, gold, oak, mahogany, velvet).

His dark materials.

He sketches the relationship between Lyra and Pantalaimon, the way they tell each other off like a brother and sister ("Behave yourself"... "Stop fussing"). Even before we turn a page, we know that their exchanges will show us Lyra's innermost feelings. And although this is a fantasy trilogy, in which many weird and wonderful things will happen, the only fantastical element in the first scene is Pantalaimon. He is given a gender, but no further explanation – just a single word, "currently", to let slip that he is a shape-shifter. Daemons are the most memorable of Pullman's creations, and he has enough confidence in them to want us to get to know them bit by bit. It's the sort of decision-making that can keep you enthralled for 1200 pages.

II How to capture a phase of life

Remember the time
When everyone was like a seal
Before the wax hardened.
Each of us bears the stamp
Of a friend met along the way –
In everyone, the trace of everyone.
For better or worse,
For wiser or sillier,
Everyone imprinted with everyone.
[Primo Levi, part of 'To My Friends', 1985, published in *The Mirror Maker*, 1990; original in Italian, translation my own]

There is an English word, impressionable, which tends to appear in only one phrase – an impressionable age, covering all the stages we go through between being a toddler and becoming an adult. This poem by Primo Levi takes that idea and runs with it, capturing the impact of our early friendships, or rather relationships of any kind, as Levi says a few lines earlier that he means friends "in the widest sense of the word – siblings, relatives, schoolmates, colleagues, lovers".

Levi keeps it beautifully simple, using much the same metaphor in three or four forms (seal, stamp, trace, imprinted), and not worrying about saying "everyone" again and again. By concentrating hard, he hits the nail on the head. Levi had seen the human race at its worst: the writing he is best known for is his testimony from Auschwitz. But here he looks back beyond that, to a happier and more widespread experience.

Poetry tends to pop up when it is most needed. I wouldn't know this poem if I hadn't lost my brother, Charlie, who dropped dead in 2014 at the age of 54. We asked a couple of his old friends to read something at his memorial service, and one of them went for this. It was an inspired choice, direct, memorable and piercingly true. Charlie was two years older than me, so I followed him to school and university; when he discovered a new enthusiasm, I tended to catch it like a bug. Sitting in the front pew listening to the poem, I thought about all the imprints he had left on me. In the words of Alan Bennett (page 76), it was as if a hand had come out and taken mine, which, at that moment, needed holding. Primo Levi's words made a deep impression on a lot of people that day. That's the one problem with the way we talk about an impressionable age: it never really ends. The wax doesn't have to harden.

III How to have fun with an obituary

The Economist, a weekly news magazine, is famous for not telling its readers the names of its writers. But there is one person on the staff whose writing is easily spotted. Every week, after spending 60 pages telling its readers that the world's problems can be solved with looser trade regulations, The Economist gives them a treat: an obituary. It's the most soulful thing in the whole magazine, sometimes the only soulful thing. The author is nearly always Ann Wroe, a biographer with a gift for getting inside the head of whoever it is that has just died. Obituaries actually have very little to do with death: they're all about capturing a life. On this occasion, it wasn't the life of a person.

> *Peterborough, in the English Midlands, is a red-brick town, best known as the midway point on the line between King's Cross and York. But from the bottom of Kingfisher Lake, just outside it, urban toil seems far away. There, all is most delightful silt and slime. A push of your probing nose sends up puffs and clouds of fine mud through the water. A riff of bubbles rises, silvery, towards the surface. The green reeds quiver, and sunlight ripples down almost to the depths where you are lurking, plump and still.*
>
> *Such was mostly the life, and such was the address, of Benson, England's most famous fish. Her actual place of birth, as a wriggling, transparent fry prey to every frog, pike and heron, was never known. But at ten, when she was stocked in Kingfisher, she was already a bruiser. And there, among the willow-shaded banks, she grew. And grew. At her peak weight, in 2006, she was 64lb 2oz (29kg), and was almost circular, like a puffed-up plaice. Bigger carp have been seen in Thailand and in France; but she still amounted to a lot of gefilte fish.*
>
> *In her glory days she reminded some of Marilyn Monroe, others of Raquel Welch. She was lither than either as she cruised through the water-weed, a lazy twist of gold.*
>
> [The Economist, 13 August 2009]

The piece gets off to a slow start: if I'd been Ann's editor, I would have (tentatively) suggested that Peterborough was a red herring. But as soon as you reach "silt and slime", you hear a voice ring out. And with "a push of your probing nose", we find that not only is the writer putting herself in the position of another species, but she's putting us there too. Like Philip Pullman a couple of pages back,

Ann Wroe uses short vivid words and staggered alliteration (silt, slime; push, probing, puffs; silvery, surface; reeds, ripples). With "a riff of bubbles", she mints a phrase, and it's a beauty, turning a sight into a sound, recasting something silent as a sequence of notes.

Ann has dropped us in the water, but she still hasn't introduced her subject. Now she does, and she puts "Benson, England's most famous fish" at the end of its sentence, for maximum impact. She shows us Benson as a baby, in a flash of Disney-ish pathos, then, more brusquely, as "a bruiser". She has some fun with Benson's dimensions, and doesn't flinch from the fact that, for us humans, carp is usually a meal. She has some more fun with the celebrities to whom Benson was compared: two Hollywood goddesses dating from the curvaceous era. Reading that sentence, I wondered why Ann had bothered with Raquel Welch, who doesn't add much to the more celebrated Marilyn Monroe. The reason becomes clear a moment later, with "she was lither than either". All the fun has been building up to this line, which takes a familiar adjective, "lithe", and carries it into the uncharted waters of the comparative, just so that it can rhyme with "either". The pleasure Ann is taking in her work has become contagious. But she is not just playing it for laughs: by the end of the sentence, she has changed gear again, going for poetry in "a lazy twist of gold".

If your library takes The Economist, slip in there on a Friday, open it at the inside back page, settle in a corner, and give yourself a five-minute masterclass.

IV How to make a modern fable

Once upon a time, a hundred years ago, there was a dark and stormy girl.

The girl was Russian, and although her hair and eyes and fingernails were dark all of the time, she was stormy only when she thought it absolutely neces-

sary. Which was fairly often.

Her name was Feodora.

She lived in a wooden house made of timber taken from the surrounding forest. The walls were layered with sheep's wool to keep out the Russian winter, and the inside was lit with hurricane lamps. Feo had painted the lamps every colour in her box of paints, so the house cast out light into the forest in reds and greens and yellows. Her mother had cut and sanded the door herself, and the wood was eight inches thick. Feo had painted it snow blue. The wolves had added claw marks over the years, which helped dissuade unwelcome visitors.

It all began – all of it – with someone knocking on the snow-blue door.

Although 'knocking' was not the right word for this particular noise, Feo thought. It sounded as though someone was trying to dig a hole in the wood with his knuckles.

But any knocking at all was unusual. Nobody knocked: it was just her and her mother and the wolves. Wolves do not knock. If they want to come in, they come in through the window, whether it is open or not.

[Katherine Rundell, *The Wolf Wilder*, 2015]

Anyone born since the mid-1980s has lived through a golden age of children's literature. When Katherine Rundell was a child living in Zimbabwe, she received a parcel for her 11th birthday: the first book about a character she had never heard of called Harry Potter. Diving into it, she found that Harry was a month older than her. "I fell in love with him," she wrote many years later, "or if not with him, because he is the least sharply drawn character, then with the secret world lying so discreetly alongside my own." When she grew up, she became a Fellow of All Souls, the Oxford college that is so clever, it doesn't have any students, just dons. She became an expert on John Donne, a very grown-up poet. But she hasn't lost her love of children's stories and now she writes them herself. This is the opening page of her second novel for children.

When you write a book for children, you have to work out what level to pitch it at, what you can trust the reader to know or to cope with. Rundell shows here that she has found a subtle answer to this question, mixing classic simplicity with modern sophistication. The language she uses is like a mountain stream, bright and clear and flowing. The first seven verbs in her story are "was", "was", "were", "was", "thought", "was" and "was". The opening words are the oldest gambit in town, "once upon a time". But there's a twist, in fact two: rather than using those words to express timelessness, as most authors do, Rundell instantly pitches her tent in a particular period, whose significance becomes clear when she adds a location. Then she plays off another familiar phrase: "there was a dark and stormy girl". In the space of one line, she has set out two stalls, suggesting that her tale will be a fable, and also a laugh. The second paragraph, after briskly introducing us to her heroine, ends on the same note of knowing humour.

The third paragraph is only four words long, which tells us that (a) Feodora is important, and (b) Rundell agrees with George Orwell, who recommended varying your paragraph length for maximum effect. The fourth paragraph is a scene setter, a little feast for the senses made up of texture (the wood and the wool) and colour (the lamps and the paints), including a shade that is deliciously fresh – every child reading this story will know snow-white, but snow-blue will be new to them.

The fourth paragraph also introduces the characters Feo lives with, in two sentences that are models of show and tell. The sentence about the door is quietly feminist, showing us that Feo's mother is ingenious and self-sufficient, with no need of a man about the house. The sentence about the wolves gets a lot of mileage out of one of the plainest words in the English language: "the".

Rundell drops in "the wolves" the way you or I might say "the dogs", and that deft little article tells us that the wolves are members of the household.

By the end of the paragraph, she is using the first word in the book that might not be in an eight-year-old's vocabulary: "dissuade". She is prepared to risk trusting her young readers a little too much, which is the right side to err on. "They can always guess," she said when asked about this at the Story Museum in Oxford. "Or ask a grown-up."

The fifth paragraph is another intensely short one. It gives us what is known in Hollywood – where this story may well end up – as the inciting incident: the event that sets the plot in motion.

During that talk, Rundell read a couple of extracts from her book, and one of them ended where this one does, with the wolves' policy on windows, which got a laugh. Sitting at the back, I witnessed another strength of her sentences: they are easy to read aloud. Although she still has a soft spot for J. K. Rowling, Rundell is closer to the Philip Pullman school of storytelling. Feo is a heroine like Lyra, fearless and resourceful. Her world mixes elements of the real and the fantastical, and the prose rattles along, delivering sophisticated suspense. The paperback of *The Wolf Wilder* comes with a single quotation on the front cover: "'A triumph' – Philip Pullman".

V How to find the middle of the bat

The Real Thing is a wise and witty play by Tom Stoppard from 1982 which has been revived every few years since. It's the story of Henry, a playwright, and Annie, an actress. They are having an affair, while married to other people, and Annie is campaigning for the release of Brodie, a young soldier who has been sent to jail for setting a wreath alight at the Cenotaph in London. When

Tom Stoppard in 1990

Brodie too tries to write a play, Annie asks Henry to be his ghost, making it more polished. Henry responds by picking up a cricket bat.

> HENRY: *Shut up and listen. This thing here, which looks like a wooden club, is actually several pieces of particular wood cunningly put together in a certain way so that the whole thing is sprung, like a dance floor. It's for hitting cricket balls with. If you get it right, the cricket ball will travel 200 yards in four seconds, and all you've done is give it a knock like knocking the top off a bottle of stout, and it makes a noise like a trout taking a fly…* (He clucks his tongue to make the noise.) *What we're trying to do is to write cricket bats, so that when we throw up an idea and give it a little knock, it might… travel…* (He clucks his tongue again and picks up the script.) *Now, what we've got here is a lump of wood of roughly the same shape trying to be a cricket bat, and if you hit a ball with it, the ball will travel about ten feet and you will drop the bat and dance about shouting 'Ouch!' with your hands stuck into your armpits.* (Indicating the cricket bat) *This isn't better because someone says it's better, or because there's a conspiracy by the MCC to keep cudgels out of Lord's. It's better because it's better. You don't believe me, so I suggest you go out to bat with this and see how you get on. 'You're a strange boy, Billy, how old are you?' 'Twenty, but I've lived more than you'll ever live.' Ooh, ouch!* (He drops the script and hops about with his hands in his armpits, going 'Ouch!' Annie watches him expressionlessly until he desists.)

Tom Stoppard, who can be dazzlingly clever, keeps it simple here ("drop the bat and dance about" ... "It's better because it's better"). The clever bit is seeing a piece of writing as a cricket bat, and not as a shot, which would be the more obvious metaphor. Henry, who is also dazzlingly clever, has been expressing everything well except passion, but he manages to show his feelings here.

Reading the speech decades later, we may find the odd note jarring: "shut up and listen" reeks of sexism, and "a bottle of stout" now summons either an old-school pub or a bunch of hipsters. If you were putting *The Real Thing* on today, you might change "stout" to "beer", thus avoiding the rhyme with "trout", which feels accidental anyway. But this is a speech that has become deservedly famous, because it expresses a vital truth about writing. Stoppard is sticking his neck out, writing something that has to be both a cri de coeur and a coherent analysis, as well as an example of what it is talking about. It has to come off the middle of the bat, and it does.

If cricket metaphors are off-putting, here's the same point wearing different clothes, and trying to practise what I preached in chapters one, two and three – be clear, be concise, be vivid.

Make it sing.

AFTERWORD

This book was dreamed up by Jon Connell, an editor who is also an inventor – of the Connell Guides and The Week magazine. Many thanks to him for trusting me with it, and to Samantha Weinberg for bringing us together. Thanks also to Nick Newman for his lovable cartoons; to Paul Woodward for his cool-headed production skills; to Jonny Patrick, Shivaun Mason and Malcolm Hebron for setting my compass; to Joe Hartley for suggesting Your Turn; to Araminta Whitley for her wise guidance; to countless colleagues for putting up with my pedantry; to Amanda, Dan and Laura for living with it; and to you, for reading.

A few final suggestions, so short that you can take a picture of them on your phone:

Keep a diary
(as irregular as you like, and private to start with)
Pick up a paper
(wouldn't it be great if someone with a good eye gave you the best stories of the day? Oh, they already do) Learn a language
(it will sharpen your English)
Join a library
("every book you find has friends it wants to introduce you to, like a party in the library that need never end" – Caitlin Moran)
Start a magazine
(every school should have one, if only a sheet of A4)

END NOTES

ANSWERS TO YOUR TURN

PAGE 35 – There's more than one way to fix this, but the simplest is to cut the words in the middle – as well as "different", which adds nothing to "variety".

One of the most attractive things about South Africa is the variety of its scenery.

PAGE 92 – All are similes except the first, which is a metaphor.

INDEX

NOTES